# Georgia

## By Carmen Bredeson

**Consultant**
Nanci Vargus, Ed. D.
Primary Multiage Teacher
Decatur Township Schools, Indianapolis, Indiana

Children's Press®
A Division of Scholastic Inc.
New York   Toronto   London   Auckland   Sydney
Mexico City   New Delhi   Hong Kong
Danbury, Connecticut

Designer: Herman Adler Design
Photo Researcher: Caroline Anderson
The photo on the cover shows part of the Okefenokee Swamp in Georgia.

**Library of Congress Cataloging-in-Publication Data**

Bredeson, Carmen.
  Georgia / by Carmen Bredeson.
    p. cm. — (Rookie read-about geography)
Includes index.
Summary: Introduces the state of Georgia, including its diverse geographical
features, agricultural crops, wildlife, cities, and famous citizens.
  ISBN 0-516-22670-3 (lib. bdg.)    0-516-27497-X (pbk.)
  1. Georgia—Juvenile literature. [1. Georgia.] I. Title. II. Series.
F286.3 .B74 2002
975.8—dc21                JE
                          BRE                2002005503
$14.25
©2002 Children's Press    C. 1
A Division of Scholastic Inc.
All rights reserved. Published simultaneously in Canada.
Printed in the United States of America.

Do you know which state
is called the Peach State?

The state of Georgia!
Georgia is located in the
southeast part of the
United States. Can you
find it on this map?

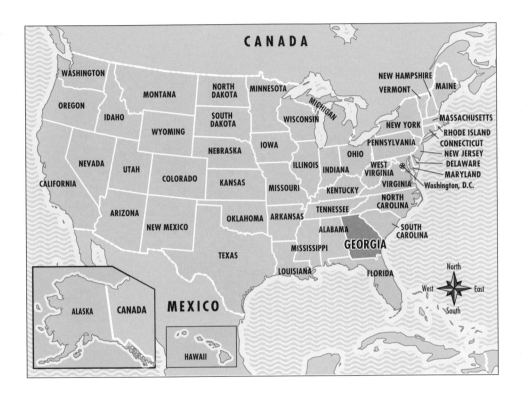

CANADA

WASHINGTON
OREGON
IDAHO
MONTANA
NORTH DAKOTA
MINNESOTA
NEW HAMPSHIRE
VERMONT
MAINE
WYOMING
SOUTH DAKOTA
WISCONSIN
MICHIGAN
NEW YORK
MASSACHUSETTS
RHODE ISLAND
CONNECTICUT
NEVADA
UTAH
NEBRASKA
IOWA
PENNSYLVANIA
NEW JERSEY
DELAWARE
CALIFORNIA
COLORADO
KANSAS
ILLINOIS
INDIANA
OHIO
WEST VIRGINIA
MARYLAND
Washington, D.C.
MISSOURI
KENTUCKY
VIRGINIA
ARIZONA
NEW MEXICO
OKLAHOMA
ARKANSAS
TENNESSEE
NORTH CAROLINA
SOUTH CAROLINA
TEXAS
MISSISSIPPI
ALABAMA
GEORGIA
LOUISIANA
FLORIDA

North
West
East
South

ALASKA
CANADA
MEXICO
HAWAII

There are mountains and waterfalls in the northern part of Georgia. The highest waterfall is called Amicalola.

The forests in Georgia have oak, poplar, and pine trees.

Brown thrashers build
nests in the tall trees.
The brown thrasher is
Georgia's state bird.

10

The weather in Georgia can be cold in the winter. Summer is always nice and warm. Plants grow well in the warm sunshine.

The land in Georgia
is good for farming.
Farmers grow cotton,
corn, peanuts, peaches,
and other important crops.

The Okefenokee Swamp is
found in southern Georgia.
The swamp is full of mud
and rotting plants.

Alligators poke their noses out of the brown water. Wood storks build nests in the trees.

Part of Georgia is next to the Atlantic Ocean. People like to visit the sandy beaches.

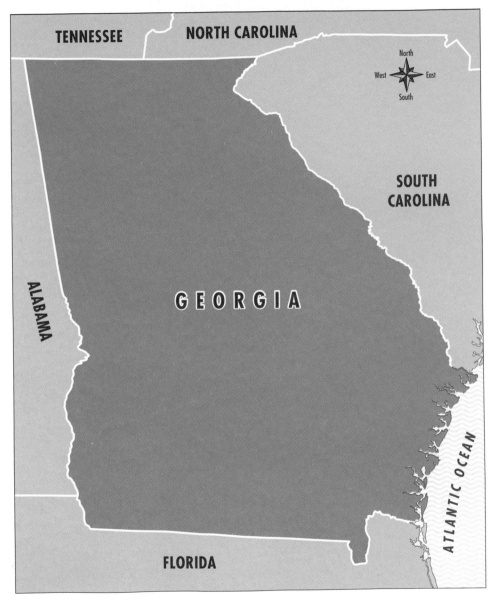

TENNESSEE

NORTH CAROLINA

SOUTH
CAROLINA

ALABAMA

GEORGIA

ATLANTIC OCEAN

FLORIDA

North
West — East
South

There are islands off the coast of Georgia. You can see wild horses, sea turtles, and many kinds of birds on these islands.

Fishermen from Georgia catch shrimp, crab, and fish in the ocean.

Atlanta is the capital of Georgia. Laws are made in the state capitol building.

23

Millions of people live in
and around Atlanta. They
work in tall office buildings,
stores, and factories.

The main office for Coca-Cola is in Atlanta. You can visit the Coca-Cola museum.

Savannah is a smaller, quieter Georgia city. Beautiful houses line the streets. Shady parks give people a place to enjoy nature.

What is your favorite
place in Georgia?

# Words You Know

Amicalola

Atlanta

beaches

brown thrasher

Okefenokee Swamp

peaches

Savannah

shrimp

31

# Index

# About the Author

Carmen Bredeson is the author of twenty-five books for children. She lives in Texas and enjoys doing research and traveling.

# Photo Credits

Photographs © 2002: David R. Frazier: 13 top, 20, 31 bottom right; H. Armstrong Roberts, Inc.: 3, 31 top right (Camerique), 29 (Joe Maher), 25 (H. Sutton); Image Bank/J. Carmichael: 6, 30 top left; Peter Arnold Inc./Jeff Greenberg: 23; Photo Researchers, NY/M.P. Kahl: 15; Stone/Getty Images: 8 (James Randklev), 24, 30 top right, (Ron Sherman); Superstock, Inc.: 26, 31 bottom left; Tom Till: cover; Transparencies, Inc.: 16, 30 bottom left (Susan K. McElveen), 19 (Jim McGuire), 14, 31 top left (Chip Padgett); Unicorn Stock Photos: 10 (Dick Keen), 11 (Martha McBride), 9, 30 bottom right (Ted Rose); Visuals Unlimited/Inga Spence: 13 bottom.

Maps by Bob Italiano